AFRICAN AMERICANS IN RADIO, FILM, AND TV ENTERTAINMENT

LINDA J. ARMSTRONG

TITLES IN THIS SERIES

AFRICAN AMERICANS IN RADIO, FILM, AND TV ENTERTAINMENT

LINDA J. ARMSTRONG

MASON CREST
PHILADELPHIA

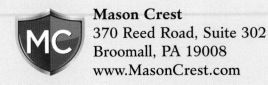

Mason Crest
370 Reed Road, Suite 302
Broomall, PA 19008
www.MasonCrest.com

Printed and bound in the United States of America.

CPSIA Compliance Information: Batch #MBC2012-10. For further information, contact Mason Crest at 1-866-MCP-Book.

First printing
1 3 5 7 9 8 6 4 2

Library of Congress Cataloging-in-Publication Data

Armstrong, Linda J.
  African Americans in radio, film, and TV entertainment / Linda J. Armstrong.
       p. cm. — (Major Black contributions from Emancipation to civil rights)
  Includes bibliographical references and index.
  ISBN 978-1-4222-2380-2 (hc)
  ISBN 978-1-4222-2393-2 (hc)
  1. African American entertainers—Biography—Juvenile literature. I. Title.
  PN2286.A76 2012
  792.092'396073—dc23
  [B]

                           2011051946

Publisher's note: All quotations in this book are taken from original sources, and contain the spelling and grammatical inconsistencies of the original texts.

Picture credits: Library of Congress: 10, 14, 17, 19, 20, 22, 36; Carl Van Vechten Photographs Collection at the Library of Congress: 40; photo by Alan Light: 49; National Aeronautics and Space Administration: 52; Columbia Pictures/Photofest: 8; NBC/Photofest: 26, 31; © 2012 Photos.com, a division of Getty Images: 16; cinemafestival / Shutterstock.com: 44; Helga Esteb / Shutterstock.com: 3, 46; Featureflash / Shutterstock.com: 7, 12, 34, 42, 45, 53, 54; Eugene Parciasepe / Shutterstock.com: 50.

TABLE OF CONTENTS

INTRODUCTION

Dr. Marc Lamont Hill

It is impossible to tell the story of America without telling the story of Black Americans. From the struggle to end slavery, all the way to the election of the first Black president, the Black experience has been a window into America's own movement toward becoming a "more perfect union." Through the tragedies and triumphs of Blacks in America, we gain a more full understanding of our collective history and a richer appreciation of our collective journey. This book series, Major Black Contributions from Emancipation to Civil Rights, spotlights that journey by showing the many ways that Black Americans have been a central part of our nation's development.

In this series, we are reminded that Blacks were not merely objects of history, swept up in the winds of social and political inevitability. Rather, since the end of legal slavery, Black men and women have actively fought for their own rights and freedoms. It is through their courageous efforts (along with the efforts of allies of all races) that Blacks are able to enjoy ever increasing levels of inclusion in American democracy. Through this series, we learn the names and stories of some of the most important contributors to our democracy.

But this series goes far beyond the story of slavery to freedom. The books in this series also demonstrate the various contributions of Black Americans to the nation's social, cultural, technological, and intellectual growth. While these books provide new and deeper insights into the lives and stories of familiar figures like Martin Luther King, Michael Jordan, and Oprah Winfrey, they also introduce readers to the contributions of countless heroes who have often been pushed to the margins of history. In reading this series, we are able to see that Blacks have been key contributors across every field of human endeavor.

Although this is a series about Black Americans, it is important and necessary reading for everyone. While readers of color will find enormous purpose and pride in uncovering the history of their ancestors, these books should also create similar sentiments among readers of all races and ethnicities. By understanding the rich and deep history of Blacks, a group often ignored or marginalized in history, we are reminded that everyone has a story. Everyone has a contribution. Everyone matters.

The insights of these books are necessary for creating deeper, richer, and more inclusive classrooms. More importantly, they remind us of the power and possibility of individuals of all races, places, and traditions. Such insights not only allow us to understand the past, but to create a more beautiful future.

This scene from *A Raisin in the Sun* features (from left) Ruby Dee (as Ruth Younger), Claudia McNeil (as Lena Younger), Diana Sands (as Beneatha Younger), and Sidney Poitier (as Walter Lee Younger).

1

A DREAM NOT DEFERRED

O n the evening of March 11, 1959, 28-year-old Lorraine Hansberry took her seat on the aisle. It was opening night in New York City for her Broadway play, *A Raisin in the Sun*. Her producer, Philip Rose, sat beside her at the Ethel Barrymore Theatre. The play had been well received at showings in New Haven, Connecticut; Philadelphia; and Chicago. However, Broadway would be a tough test. It was, and still is, known as the nation's leading theater district.

The outlook didn't look especially promising. A preview the night before had received mixed reviews. Hansberry and Rose weren't expecting much more on opening night. Although they believed their play portrayed real African-American characters and not stereotypes, they were unsure how the story would be received by the mostly white audience at the Ethel Barrymore Theatre.

While they didn't realize it at the time, that opening night would change their lives. It would change the lives of cast members. It would even make a difference for all African Americans.

TRIUMPH!

The lights went down and the curtain rose to show the Younger family gathered in a dingy room. They had just received good news that they were getting a check for $10,000. The father had died and the money was his life insurance.

> **— Did You Know? —**
>
> The title of Lorraine Hansberry's groundbreaking play comes from "Harlem," a poem by the African-American poet Langston Hughes.

Each family member wanted to spend the money in a different way. The mother always dreamed of having a bigger home for her family. So she put money down on a house. The house was perfect, except for one thing: it was in a white neighborhood. The neighbors didn't want the Youngers to live there.

Lorraine Hansberry

When the play's powerful first act ended, the curtain fell. Behind the curtain, the actors heard silence. As cast member Louis Gossett Jr. later wrote, they feared that they had failed. Instead, the silence broke and there was a roar of applause.

After the second act, the applause lasted longer. At the end of the play, there were 15 curtain calls. Everyone was standing and clapping. Even the critics stayed. The audience kept calling, "Author! Author!" But Hansberry stayed in her seat. The cast wasn't sure what to do. So Ruby Dee, who played Ruth Younger, urged Sidney Poitier, who played Walter Lee Younger, to get Hansberry. Poitier jumped off the stage, dashed up the aisle and half-carried the young playwright to join the cast.

CHANGING AMERICAN THEATER

Reviews for *A Raisin in the Sun* were stunning. *New York Age*, an African-American newspaper in Harlem, told its readers, "Don't go to see this play

only because a Negro wrote it, a Negro directed it, it's about Negroes, and Negroes act in it. Go to see it because it's one of the most moving experiences you'll ever have in the theater."

A Raisin in the Sun ran for almost two years on Broadway. It won the

The Story Behind the Play

Lorraine Hansberry drew on personal experience when writing *A Raisin in the Sun*. In 1937, her family bought a house in a white neighborhood in Chicago. They were greeted with hostility. White neighbors constantly threatened and harassed the Hansberrys, hoping to get them to move. The white residents also tried to use the legal system to force the Hansberrys out. Property owners in the neighborhood weren't supposed to sell to African Americans as part of an agreement called a "restrictive covenant."

Carl Hansberry, Lorraine's father, was a real estate broker. He was determined to fight restrictive covenants in the courts. He believed that the issue was bigger than just his family. It was about discrimination against all African Americans. Carl Hansberry took the case all the way to the United States Supreme Court. In 1940, the Supreme Court decided in favor of Hansberry. It ruled that restrictive covenants were illegal.

That decision didn't make the Hansberry family any more welcome in their neighborhood. Nor did it eliminate racial discrimination in housing. Still, it was a major step.

In writing *A Raisin in the Sun*, Lorraine Hansberry hoped to do more than make a statement against racism and discrimination. "I think it will help a lot of people to understand how we [blacks] are just as complicated as they are—and just as mixed up—but above all, that we have among our . . . ranks people who are the very essence of human dignity," Hansberry explained in a letter to her mother.

Tragically, Hansberry's career was cut short by cancer. She died in January 1965. She was just 34.

Actor Louis Gossett Jr., a member of the original 1959 cast of *A Raisin in the Sun*, went on to have a distinguished acting career.

New York Drama Critics' Circle Award for 1959's best play. *A Raisin in the Sun* was later made into movies for the big screen and for television. The big-screen version, released in 1961, featured the original Broadway cast. Claudia McNeil and Sidney Poitier were nominated for Golden Globe Awards. Ruby Dee received the National Board of Review Award for Supporting Actress. A decade later, in 1974, *Raisin*, a musical based on the play, won a Tony Award for Best Musical.

A Raisin in the Sun hit Broadway again in 2004 with a new set of stars, including Phylicia Rashad and Sean "Diddy" Combs. The revival received four Tony nominations. Rashad became the first African-American woman to win Leading Actress in a Play honors. Audra McDonald took the award for Best Actress in a Featured Role.

DREAMS COMING TRUE

The play's success put several members of the 1959 cast on the road to stardom. Sidney Poitier, who played the son in the original production, later earned an Academy Award for Best Actor for *Lilies of the Field* (1963). "I knew for certain I was meant to be an actor," Poitier wrote in his 2000 book, *The Measure of a Man: A Spiritual Autobiography*, "when the curtain came down on opening night in New York. . . . After all the years of struggling with a craft I couldn't get a grip on . . . I was an actor."

Louis Gossett Jr. also went on to win an Academy Award. Gossett took home Best Supporting Actor honors for his role in 1982's *An Officer and a Gentleman*. For Gossett, *A Raisin in the Sun* remained relevant long after its original run. "One line in the play, 'Seem like God didn't see fit to give

the Black man nothing but dreams,' stayed in my head long after the play closed, as I found myself one of the blessed whose dreams were coming true," Gossett wrote in his 2010 autobiography, *An Actor and a Gentleman*.

The triumph of *A Raisin in the Sun* was a high point in American theater. It was also a milestone in

=== Did You Know? ===

The first Tony Awards ceremony was held in 1947. The prize was named after Antoinette Perry, an actress, director, and producer. During World War II, Perry headed the American Theatre Wing, which entertained servicemen.

the history of African-Americans in the performing arts. Thousands of gifted actors, singers, dancers, and writers have been part of that long history. With this book, you'll learn about a few of them. It is a tale of courage and genius in the face of ignorance and fear.

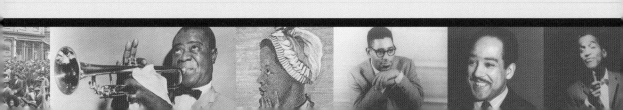

MR. IRA ALDRIDGE AS AARON.

" He dies upon my scimetar's sharp point,

This playbill from a London theater shows the African-American actor Ira Aldridge (1807–1867) playing the role of Aaron in Shakepeare's *Titus Andronicus*, circa 1852.

2

TAKING THE STAGE

A play like *A Raisin in the Sun* would never have been recognized as great if it weren't for the hard work and determination of earlier African-American actors and playwrights. One of those pioneering actors was Ira Aldridge. In 1821, as a teenager, he attended the African Grove Theater in New York City. The 300-seat theater presented amateur productions of plays by William Shakespeare. Unlike other theaters of the time that did Shakespeare's plays, the African Grove used African-American actors. Its audiences, too, were mostly black.

One of the stars of the African Grove Theater was James Hewlett. He became famous for playing Othello, the title character of one of Shakespeare's best tragedies. Though the character is black, Hewlett was apparently the first black man to play Othello.

Inspired by Hewlett, the young Ira Aldridge decided to pursue a career as an actor. But his father, a minister, didn't like the idea. He sent his son to study at the University of Glasgow in Scotland. However, Aldridge soon traveled to London to act. English audiences loved him. He played Othello in the early 1830s and added many other roles later. For 30 years, Aldridge toured Europe, where he was one of the most acclaimed actors. He even performed for kings and queens. Royal courts in many countries showered him with honors.

This 19th-century illustration depicts the death of the slave known as "Uncle Tom" in the Harriet Beecher Stowe novel. The book was very popular, and helped raise support for ending slavery in the South. This would increase tensions between the Northern and Southern states in the 1850s, and lead to the start of the Civil War in April 1861.

Aldridge never returned to the United States, where African Americans faced discrimination, and roles for black actors were rare. He died in 1867.

UNCLE TOM'S CABIN

In 1852, a white abolitionist named Harriet Beecher Stowe published *Uncle Tom's Cabin*. The anti-slavery novel sold more than 300,000 copies. In the North, it helped stir up opposition to slavery. In the slave states of the South, the book provoked rage.

Uncle Tom's Cabin inspired a host of stage productions that featured scenes from the bestseller. These "Tom shows," as they were called, were extremely popular. More than a million people saw one of them. Tom shows were even staged in the South, where they were adapted to express a pro-slavery message.

Tom shows helped shape the way many people thought about African Americans. Although many of the characters were black, white actors played all the parts. They darkened their faces and hands with burnt cork. The enslaved characters in Tom shows were all very one-dimensional. They resembled cartoons more than real people. Uncle Tom—loyal, gentle, and God-fearing—submitted patiently to his servitude. Mammy was a loving cook. Sam was lazy and happy.

The Tom shows didn't go away after the Civil War: a few were around as late as the 1940s and 1950s. The stereotypes of black people presented in the Tom shows also lingered. For a long time, black actors who wanted

These posters for 19th century productions of *Uncle Tom's Cabin* show two different, but equally unrealistic, portrayals of African Americans. The top poster (1898) shows caricatures with offensively exaggerated features. On the lower poster (1881), the African-American character Eliza displays an almost supernatural determination—and appears to be white.

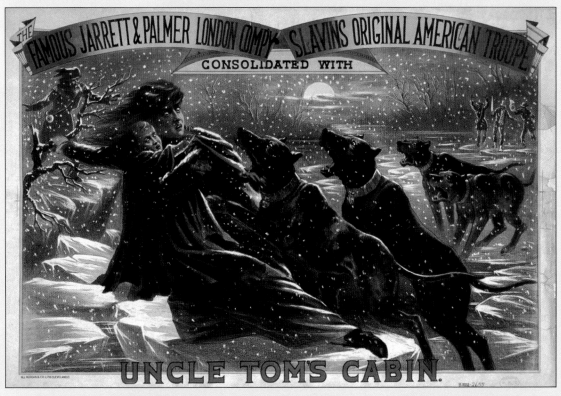

to work had to take similar parts. In plays and movies, they portrayed warm-hearted maids like Mammy, loyal servants like Uncle Tom, and happy-go-lucky losers like Sam.

BLACKFACE AND MINSTREL SHOWS

Minstrel shows were a form of popular entertainment that started in the 1830s. These shows featured songs, dances, and jokes—some of which were borrowed from African-American traditions. The first minstrel shows didn't involve African Americans, though. Instead, as with the Tom shows, white actors portrayed African Americans by wearing makeup called black-face. Minstrel comics dressed in baggy clothes, spoke with a strange accent, and acted foolish. White audiences in the North thought they were funny and enjoyed the songs and dances.

After the Civil War, many African-American entertainers joined min-strel troupes. These touring groups gave numerous talented performers their start.

By the early 1900s, the popularity of minstrel shows had faded. Still,

Tom Show Favorites

Each "Tom show" was different. However, some scenes were almost always included. One of them was the escape of the slave Eliza and her young son.

In the scene, the frightened mother reaches the banks of the Ohio River. She sees no way to cross. A slave dealer and his dogs are closing in. Clutching her son, the desperate Eliza jumps onto an ice floe in the river. Then she jumps from that ice floe to another, and then to another. In this manner, Eliza manages to cross the river safely with her son.

Audiences loved the scene, which is depicted in the poster at the bottom of page 17. They often cheered Eliza on as she made her escape.

This poster for a 19th century minstrel show includes pictures of four white comedians wearing blackface makeup. The stereotyped "black" characters played by white actors in minstrel shows contributed to racism by spreading negative images of African Americans.

elements of minstrelsy had been incorporated into another successful form of stage entertainment: vaudeville. Vaudeville shows featured a variety of acts, including singers, dancers, and comedians.

BERT WILLIAMS: A SAD, FUNNY MAN

Blackface makeup was degrading to African-American people. Yet some black minstrels and vaudeville entertainers wore it anyway. At the time, there simply weren't many options for African-American performers.

One African American who performed in blackface ranks among the most talented entertainers of the early 1900s. When Bert Williams did pantomime, he conveyed a sense of pure joy. Behind the makeup, however, was a man deeply wounded by the racism he constantly endured. The great vaudeville performer W. C. Fields called Williams "the funniest man I ever saw and the saddest man I ever knew."

Williams was born in the Bahamas in 1874. When he was 11, his parents brought their family to the United States in search of economic opportunity. They settled in Riverside, California.

At school in the United States, Bert Williams was the class clown. He loved to make his friends laugh. He was also gifted musically, learning to

Bert Williams (left, in blackface makeup) and his longtime comedy partner George Walker (1873–1911). This photo was taken to promote their popular 1903 musical *In Dahomey*.

play the piano by ear. When he was 16, he worked in a medicine show. These traveling sales events were very popular. They involved fake doctors who charged high prices for pills and potions. The shows used entertainment to attract customers. Williams stood outside the show's big tent. It was his job to attract a crowd. He made the event inside sound exciting. Next, Williams joined a musical group. He performed at a hotel near his home.

These experiences taught Williams something important: he liked entertaining people, and he was good at it. He headed for San Francisco, the theater center of California. There, Williams met George Walker, who had also worked for medicine shows. The two young men became partners and worked in a minstrel group for a while.

Then they took an unusual acting job. It was at the 1894 San Francisco Midwinter Exposition. The exposition's organizers had hired tribesmen from the West African country of Dahomey to perform. But the men from Dahomey hadn't yet arrived at the time of the exposition's opening, so the organizers hired Williams and Walker to play West Africans for a few days. When the real West Africans did show up, Williams and Walker enjoyed spending time with them. They decided to do a show about African culture someday.

After the exposition, the pair went to Los Angeles. Later they traveled to Colorado's booming mining towns. Working when they could as Williams & Walker, they kept heading east. A producer who spotted them at a hotel in Indiana asked the duo to perform at the Casino Theater in New York.

MUSICALS AND "THE FOLLIES"

Their act was a hit in New York. Williams and Walker went on to star in their own popular musicals. *In Dahomey*, produced in 1903, was first. Next came *Abyssinia* (1906) and *Bandana Land* (1908). African-American writers penned most of the stories, the music, and the lyrics. Williams and Walker have been called the most successful comedy team of their time.

In 1909, Walker became very ill, so Williams had to work on his own. A year later, the showman Florenz Ziegfeld offered Williams a spot in his famous *Ziegfeld Follies*. Williams starred in this variety show for many years, but he missed being in musicals. He left the *Ziegfeld Follies* in 1920. Two years later, he was performing in *Under the Bamboo Tree* when he collapsed onstage. He died at home in New York on March 4, 1922.

> — *Did You Know?* —
>
> The Williams and Walker musical *In Dahomey* was about African Americans pretending to be natives of Africa at a fair. The play opened in 1903 and quickly became a hit. Williams and Walker took the show to London. Its seven-month run there included a performance for the Prince of Wales at Buckingham Palace.

Some African-American actors didn't like the way Bert Williams used his talent. They didn't want him to wear blackface and to play the fool. Williams thought about this, too. "When we picture the negro on the stage we think of him singing, laughing, and cutting up," he told an interviewer:

> That seems to be his nature. But has it ever occurred to you that under his mask of smiles and this cloak of capers there is hidden dire tragedy? God surely has been good to the black man to make him take his lot with a smile on his face and a joke on his lips.

Still, Williams believed in the power of the theater. He thought it could change people. "Companies of purposeful players will not only uplift the black man," he said, "but they will, through the presentation of proper plays, aid toward a more perfect understanding between the races."

The great African-American actor Paul Robeson (1898–1976) plays Othello in a 1943 Broadway production of the Shakespeare play. According to the *New York Times*, Robeson "gave to the role a majesty and power that had seldom if ever been seen on the American stage."

Some people didn't find this belief too far-fetched. "Bert Williams," observed the famous African-American educator Booker T. Washington, "has done more for the race than I have. He has smiled his way into people's hearts. I have been obliged to fight my way."

PAUL ROBESON: A FORCE FOR CHANGE

Like Bert Williams, the great African-American singer, actor, and political activist Paul Robeson thought that art could change society. Born in 1898, Robeson grew up in Princeton, New Jersey. He was the son of a former slave.

At the age of 17, Robeson won a scholarship to Rutgers University. There he excelled athletically and academically. Robeson was a football, basketball, baseball, and track star. He was a member of the Phi Beta Kappa honor society and graduated at the top of his class.

In 1923, Robeson earned a law degree from Columbia University. He secured a position at a New York City law firm. But, disgusted by the racism he encountered there, he quit.

Robeson enjoyed acting, which he had been doing since high school. In 1922, Robeson had even appeared in a Broadway play. Now he decided to abandon the law in favor of a career on the stage.

In 1924, Robeson landed the lead role in *All God's Chillun Got Wings*, a play by Eugene O'Neill. It was about an African-American man married to a white woman—a daring subject for the time. In 1925, Robeson performed in another play by O'Neill, *The Emperor Jones*. It had been made famous by another great African-American actor, Charles Gilpin, five years earlier. The play was about an African-American man who escapes from prison. He goes to an island in the Caribbean and turns himself into a king. Robeson's performances in the two O'Neill plays made him a star.

CITIZEN OF THE WORLD

In 1928, Robeson went to London and performed in *Show Boat*. One tune from that musical, "Ol' Man River," would become Robeson's signature song throughout his career.

Returning to the United States, Robeson played Othello on Broadway. His performance was a sensation, and the 1930 production set a record as the longest-running Shakespeare play ever performed on Broadway.

Robeson visited the Soviet Union in 1934. He came away impressed at what he believed was the fair and decent treatment of ethnic minorities in that country. Robeson publicly praised the Soviet Union. Such statements were controversial. The Soviet Union's communist system was opposed to the capitalist systems of the United States and other Western nations. Later, Robeson's apparent sympathy for communism would ruin his career.

During the 1930s and early 1940s, Robeson worked on about a dozen films, either as an actor or a singer. He also became increasingly involved in politics. He frequently spoke out against segregation in the United States.

In the late 1940s, the United States became gripped by a fear of communism. Some American politicians suggested that Paul Robeson was a member of the Communist Party and thus a danger to the United States. In 1950, the U.S. government took away Robeson's passport. This meant he couldn't travel to other countries to perform. At the same time, Robeson found that American movie and theater producers were unwilling to hire him because of the anti-communist hysteria. But Robeson refused to be silenced. He continued to speak out for the causes he believed in, including racial justice.

In 1958, Robeson's passport was finally returned to him. He moved to Great Britain. Londoners welcomed him back to the stage, and he received many honors.

By 1963, Robeson was ill. He returned to the United States to retire. He died in Philadelphia on January 23, 1976.

Paul Robeson's son later summed up the importance of his brilliant and remarkably talented father. "The extraordinary achievements and impressive nobility of Paul Robeson," wrote Paul Robeson Jr., "made an indelible imprint on the history of the twentieth century, and his unshakable belief in the oneness of humankind inspired people all over the world."

NEW DIRECTIONS

During the 1960s, African-American playwrights and actors made audiences think about civil rights and other issues affecting black people. Langston Hughes—who was already one of the most accomplished African-American writers—broke new ground with *Black Nativity* (1961) and *Jericho-Jim Crow* (1964). These plays took the form of black gospel musicals. *Black Nativity* retold the story of the birth of Jesus, with an all-black cast. *Jericho-Jim Crow* was a tribute to the civil rights movement.

Another famous black writer, James Baldwin, produced *Blues for Mister Charlie* in 1964. The play was based on the brutal lynching of Emmett Till, an African-American teenager. That murder had taken place in Mississippi in 1955.

LeRoi Jones (who later changed his name to Amiri Baraka) wrote a number of plays that were presented "off-Broadway," in small theaters in New York. The most acclaimed, and most controversial, was 1964's *Dutchman*. It depicts an encounter between a cruel white woman and a young black man in a subway car. The play ends with the white woman murdering the black man.

During the 1970s and beyond, the concerns of African-American women were increasingly visible on the stage. A notable example is Ntozake Shange's *For Colored Girls Who Have Considered Suicide When the Rainbow Is Enuf*. The award-winning play, first staged in 1975, was made into a movie in 2010.

Hattie McDaniel (1895–1952) performs on NBC radio, 1942. McDaniel was the first African-American woman to sing on the radio, and the first black to win an Academy Award.

3

ON THE AIR

Until the 1920s, the only way to take in a concert, play, or some other kind of show was to go to a public venue such as a theater. With the coming of radio, however, people could listen to professional entertainment from their own homes.

In 1920, KDKA of Pittsburgh became the first commercial radio station to receive a broadcast license. At first, only a few hundred people heard its broadcasts, or those of the handful of other radio stations on the air. In 1920, few people had radio receivers.

The growth of radio was rapid. By 1922, some 30 stations were broadcasting around the United States, and 100,000 radio receivers were purchased. By 1923, there were more than 550 U.S. radio stations, and half a million Americans bought receivers.

In the mid-1920s, small radio stations across the country began joining chains or networks. Sponsors paid for the shows these networks broadcast. In return, they had a chance to discuss their products on the air.

Radio had great influence. It changed family life in the United States. Every evening, many families gathered around their radio to listen to news, sports, comedies, mysteries, adventures, and children's shows.

HATTIE MCDANIEL: THE STAR WHO PLAYED A MAID

In the early days of radio, most of the performers were white. A few African-American actors did star in popular programs, however. Unfortunately, most of them had to take parts as servants, pretenders, or bums. These stereotyped roles were familiar. They were like the characters in minstrel routines and Tom shows.

Hattie McDaniel was a talented African-American entertainer who would make her mark in radio before going on to a distinguished film career. Born in 1895 in Wichita, Kansas, she was the youngest of 13 children in her family. Both her parents were former slaves. Her father had served in the Union army during the Civil War.

When Hattie was five, the McDaniel family moved to Denver. At the time, African Americans often encountered less hostility in western parts of the country, and Denver had a growing black community. Hattie's mother found work as a maid in the homes of rich white families. She sometimes took her youngest daughter to work with her. Hattie learned how to cook and clean, skills her mother believed she would need when she grew up.

Two of Hattie's brothers, meanwhile, made extra money by dancing at special events with some of their friends. Later the brothers set up a black minstrel troupe and took part in touring shows.

Hattie had always loved entertaining. One day when she was eight, her brother Otis took her to a carnival. The two of them sang and danced, and the crowds threw money their way. The pair took five dollars home to their family. It was almost as much as her father earned from his pension in a whole month.

FIRSTS

At age 15, Hattie McDaniel dropped out of high school to perform in minstrel shows. She wrote songs for a group that included one of her sisters. Soon McDaniel was touring the United States with a jazz orchestra that performed on the vaudeville circuit.

In 1925, McDaniel sang on station KOA in Denver. She may have been the first African-American woman ever heard on network radio. She would achieve other firsts during her career.

With the stock market crash of 1929 and the onset of the Great Depression, millions of Americans lost their jobs. Vaudeville died. For a while, Hattie McDaniel could only find work as a bathroom attendant at a nightclub in Milwaukee, Wisconsin. After discovering her vocal talents, however, the club's owner hired her as a singer.

In 1931, McDaniel decided to move to California. She had a brother and sister there. Sam, her brother, was a local celebrity in Los Angeles. He starred in *The Optimistic Do-Nuts*, a popular radio comedy produced by station KNX. Sam McDaniel gave his sister a small part on the show. Listeners were immediately delighted by the character Hi-Hat Hattie. Soon Hattie McDaniel had replaced her brother as the star of *The Optimistic Do-Nuts*.

> ═ *Did You Know?* ═
>
> In 1930, about 40 percent of homes in the United States had radios. By 1939, the number had risen to 80 percent.

Within a year, McDaniel was being offered movie roles. During the 1930s, she acted in dozens of films. She almost always played a maid or cook, and most of the roles were comic.

In 1939, McDaniel appeared in *Gone with the Wind*. The epic is widely considered one of the best films ever. McDaniel made history in her role as the feisty house servant Mammy. She became the first African American to win an Academy Award.

TOUGH CHOICES

Not everyone in the African-American community celebrated McDaniel's success. The slaves in *Gone with the Wind* were portrayed as happy and devoted to their masters. This reinforced the notion that African Americans hadn't really minded slavery. And McDaniel was criticized not just for appearing in *Gone with the Wind*, but also for taking so many movie

roles as a servant. Unfortunately, these types of roles were the only ones available to her. "I can be a maid for $7 a week," McDaniel would say, "or I can play a maid for $700 a week."

By the late 1940s, McDaniel was finding it difficult to find movie roles even as a maid. So she returned to radio. In 1947, she became the star of a popular family comedy, *The Beulah Show*. She played a maid. Still, it was the first time a black woman had her own network show.

In 1950, Beulah moved to the newest medium: television. McDaniel filmed a few shows for the TV series, but they never aired. Her health was failing, and she couldn't work. She died of cancer on October 26, 1952.

More than 5,000 people—black and white—came to her funeral. McDaniel had asked to be buried at Hollywood Memorial Park Cemetery. But officials turned her request down because the cemetery was for whites only. She was buried at Rosedale Cemetery in Los Angeles.

EDDIE ANDERSON: JACK BENNY'S VALET

During the golden age of radio, other African-American actors starred in popular comedies. One such star was Eddie Anderson. The son of a black minstrel entertainer and a tightrope walker, Anderson started performing when he was 14. He appeared in vaudeville before landing dozens of small parts in films.

In 1937, Anderson got a big break. He was hired to perform on the radio show of Jack Benny, a popular white comedian. Anderson played the role of Benny's valet, Rochester Van Jones. At first, the character was the butt of jokes based on the same kind of racial stereotypes common in the old-time minstrel shows. Rochester was lazy. He was irresponsible. He thought he was smarter than he actually was. Even on the radio, blackface-style comedy was hard to miss.

Over time, however, the character of Rochester evolved. Rochester poked fun at the flaws of his boss. He sometimes outsmarted the white characters. This represented progress in the depiction of blacks in the entertainment field. And it came thanks largely to the superb comic talents of Eddie Anderson.

Eddie "Rochester" Anderson (1905–1977) performs on Jack Benny's radio show, 1941. Anderson played the Rochester character on the radio and television from 1937 until the mid-1960s; he also appeared in more than 60 movies.

EDDIE GREEN AND DUFFY'S TAVERN

Another popular radio show star of the 1940s was Eddie Green. Green became interested in show business while in high school. At a talent show, he told some jokes to go along with his magic act. The theater manager gave him a job, but told him to drop the tricks. "You're a comedian," he said.

Green worked at the Cotton Club, a famous nightclub in Harlem. Later, he landed a spot on Rudy Vallee's radio show. Ed Gardner, the producer of a popular show called *Duffy's Tavern*, noticed his talents and gave Green the part of the waiter on his show. Green's character was the only sensible person in the place. The show's writers made an effort to avoid racist situations.

A reporter from *Ebony* once asked Green about African Americans in radio. "We have to get in there first, then change their minds," Green said. "You can't stand outside and tell them what to do. It's their property. If you say no, they can get someone else."

BIG CHANGES IN RADIO

With the advent of television in the 1950s, more and more people started watching dramas and comedies on the little screen. Many radio shows moved to TV. People still listened to radio, but for different reasons. Some of the new radio stars played records. Others presented the news, or described the action at sporting events.

Art Rust Jr. was a pioneer sportscaster on the radio. Rust had loved baseball since his boyhood in Harlem during the 1930s. "At one time I wanted to be a major league ballplayer, but I was black," he wrote in 1976. Instead of playing professionally, Rust attended Long Island University. He got his first radio job in 1954 with a show called *The Schaefer Circle of Sports*. It was broadcast on radio station WWRL in New York. Rust later moved on to do sports and news broadcasting at other stations.

In 1981, he took the microphone at WABC, a radio station in New York. His *Sportstalk* show was a huge success. On the show, he interviewed sports figures, and listeners called in with questions. Rust wasn't the first

to try this format. But with his warm personality and deep knowledge of sports history, he earned the respect of fans and colleagues and was later referred to as "the godfather of sports talk radio."

Art Rust died on January 12, 2010. He was 82.

CHUCK LEONARD: DISC JOCKEY

Chuck Leonard was another important African-American on-air personality. His specialty was playing recorded music. He got interested in radio while attending the University of Illinois. He became program director of the university's radio station.

In 1965, Leonard took a job at WABC in New York City, becoming the first African-American DJ at a major Top 40 station. With energy and wit, he introduced and played the most popular songs in the country. He stayed there until 1979.

After that, Leonard hosted shows on several stations in the New York area. He enjoyed talking about many kinds of music, but he loved rhythm and blues. When satellite radio emerged, he joined two channels: Swing Street and Soul Review.

Leonard died on August 12, 2004, at the age of 67.

In March 2002, actress Halle Berry became the first African-American woman to win an Oscar for Best Actress for her performance in *Monster's Ball*. Denzel Washington won the Oscar for Best Actor that year for his work in *Training Day*; Washington had previously won an Oscar for Best Supporting Actor in 1989.

4

THE SILVER SCREEN

Motion pictures grew out of a scientific discovery. If a series of single pictures are shown quickly, the figures in the pictures seem to move. At first, moving pictures were shown in machines called Kinetoscopes. A viewer could look through a peephole to watch a movie. These early shows were a little more than a minute long. When moving frames were combined with projectors—which occurred in the 1890s—the way was paved for the film industry. The first permanent movie theater opened in 1896 in Buffalo, New York.

The first movies were short and simple. They were shot in black and white. These films were also silent. An organist or pianist in the theater played music to match the action on the screen.

Moviemakers wanted people to come to their shows, so they chose subjects that were already popular. Some of the first movies were versions of *Uncle Tom's Cabin*. Edwin S. Porter made one of the first versions in 1903. It was 12 minutes long. The starring actor was a white man in blackface makeup. Other versions followed in 1909 and 1913, also featuring white actors in blackface.

A DISTURBING FILM

In 1915, pioneering film director and producer D. W. Griffith released the first American blockbuster film, *The Birth of a Nation*. The film ran for more than three hours and cost $100,000 to make. At the time, that was a huge sum, equal to millions of dollars today. Griffith developed many new film effects. He used close-ups, dramatic lighting, and special cuts. The movie was an amazing piece of work for its time. In fact, other directors continue to use Griffith's techniques to tell stories through film.

While the film techniques were advanced, the story itself was not. The movie was about life in the South before and after the Civil War. In *The Birth of a Nation*, white Southerners and their slaves were happy before the war. Afterward, "bad" blacks (played in the film by white actors in blackface) and Northerners created trouble in the South. To set things right, a group called the Ku Klux Klan was formed. Clad in white hoods and robes, the Klansmen went out and restored order.

The Birth of a Nation was a fictional story. Actual events in the South after the Civil War had been much different from what Griffith's film showed. The Ku Klux Klan was a hate group that terrorized and murdered many innocent black people in the South. Its real goal was to prevent African Americans from becoming equal members of society. Nevertheless, many white people who saw *The Birth of a Nation* believed the depiction of heroic Klansmen meting out justice. They believed the portrayal of evil black men who preyed on innocent white victims, especially women. Following the film's release, the Ku Klux Klan enjoyed a resurgence of popularity across the country.

PROTESTS

When *The Birth of a Nation* was shown in New York, a recently formed civil rights organization, the National Association for the Advancement of Colored People (NAACP), picketed the theater. Large protests followed in other cities. Five states and 19 cities banned the film.

The Birth of a Nation made a lot of money. But film producers were alarmed by the backlash the film created. For decades afterward, movie studios mostly avoided portraying black men as dangerous villains. Instead, writes film historian Donald Bogle, "black males in Hollywood films were cast almost always in comic roles."

The first important motion picture with sound—known at the time as a "talkie"—was *The Jazz Singer*. It brought back the old minstrel tradition. The star was Al Jolson, a famous white entertainer, who appeared in black-face. The movie opened in 1927. It was a huge hit. Filmmakers soon started looking for singing and dancing talent to showcase in musicals. Some of the entertainers they chose were African Americans.

STEPIN FETCHIT

During the 1930s, African Americans in films, as in radio, took their places as maids and butlers. The most successful black movie actor of the time was Lincoln Theodore Monroe Andrew Perry, who used the stage name Stepin Fetchit. Perry was a remarkably gifted performer. He was also highly intelligent and well read. But the servants he played as Stepin Fetchit were stupid, lazy, and foolish. This made him an object of scorn for many African Americans.

Stepin Fetchit remains controversial today. His performances are still seen as degrading to black people—so much so that when one of his movies is shown on TV, his entire performance is usually edited out. Many African

Americans regard Stepin Fetchit as a sellout. Yet that isn't the view of everyone. Some historians have pointed out that the actor actually undermined racism in several ways. For instance, when a script called for him to say things he found offensive, Stepin Fetchit would mumble or skip over the lines in question. And this much cannot be disputed: he was hugely successful in the movie industry. Appearing in several dozen films during the 1930s, he became a millionaire. He owned six homes and a dozen cars. He, a black man, had servants.

By the 1940s, however, Hollywood had tired of Stepin Fetchit's act. Though he was no longer making much money, he continued to maintain a lavish lifestyle. He was soon bankrupt. He died in 1985.

OSCAR MICHEAUX: FILMS FOR AFRICAN AMERICANS

In the 1920s and 1930s, Hollywood producers cast African Americans in roles that white audiences expected to see. Meanwhile, independent black filmmakers were making "race films." These movies with all-black casts were made for African Americans. Oscar Micheaux was one of the film-making pioneers. He was born January 2, 1884. His parents, both former slaves, owned a small farm in Illinois.

As a young man, Micheaux used money he earned as a Pullman porter to buy his own land. When he lost it, he wrote a novel about his problems. He published his book, *The Homesteader*, himself. Then he sold the book door-to-door. His charm made him a good salesman. People enjoyed the book. In 1917, an African-American film company wanted to adapt the book into a movie.

Micheaux thought a lot of money should be spent on the filming of his novel. The film company had different ideas, so he decided to make the movie himself. That was the beginning of his career as a motion-picture producer and director. His first film, *The Homesteader*, appeared in 1919.

His second film was one of his most important. It was called *Within Our Gates*. Released in 1920, the film was made as an answer to *The Birth of a Nation*. It showed the ugly truth about slavery and the Ku Klux Klan.

Because of Micheaux's charm, people he met in his travels across the country helped fund his movies. Many of them were ordinary farmers and businessmen. Micheaux could never raise as much money as D. W. Griffith. In his own way, however, he was just as creative. He used what he had. He made many of his films in the homes of friends.

Micheaux was a one-man studio. He wrote the stories, did his own casting (often using amateur actors), and directed. Instead of depending on a distributor, he went to exhibitors personally. He convinced theater owners to run matinees for African Americans in their towns. When possible, he delivered the movies to theaters in person. Sometimes the owners gave him money for his next project.

Micheaux's later films were talkies and used professional black actors from New York. Some of them were musicals. His last movie appeared in 1948. In all, he made more than 40 films, but only 15 still exist.

Micheaux's movies have some technical flaws. Yet his work is considered an important part of American cinematic history. Micheaux presented a diverse array of black characters that matched the diversity of the African-American community. His characters weren't lazy, bumbling servants. Many were professionals such as teachers and doctors. Some were gangsters and gamblers.

Micheaux made entertainment for an audience Hollywood didn't recognize. He also filmed stories about prejudice and marriage between whites and blacks. He was a man far ahead of his time. Oscar Micheaux died of heart failure on March 25, 1951. In 1987, a star was placed, in his honor, on Hollywood's Walk of Fame.

SIDNEY POITIER

Like Oscar Micheaux, actor Sidney Poitier would be honored with a star on Hollywood's Walk of Fame. Unlike the pioneering director, Poitier would be recognized during his lifetime.

Sidney Poitier was born in Miami, Florida, on February 20, 1927. He grew up in the Bahamas. His father was a farmer. When the family moved from a small island to the Bahamian capital of Nassau, Poitier fell in love

with movies. He wanted to act. At 15, he joined his brother in Miami. A year later, he went to New York.

Poitier tried out for a part at the American Negro Theater. But his Caribbean accent was hard to understand. The director sent the young man on his way.

In the meantime, Poitier washed dishes in a café to earn a living. When he had time, he listened to the radio. He used it to practice his American accent. He also started cleaning the American Negro Theater. In exchange, he received acting lessons.

Poitier's big break came in 1945. One night during the run of a play called *Days of Our Youth*, Harry Belafonte, the lead actor, was unable to perform. As Belafonte's understudy, Poitier filled in. That performance led to a small part in another play. The critics were impressed, and more offers came Poitier's way. He appeared in numerous plays until 1950.

Harry Belafonte Jr. (b. 1927) was the first African American to win an Emmy Award, the most prestigious award for television production. The talented actor and singer was very active in the Civil Rights Movement of the 1950s and 1960s.

That year, Poitier's career shifted to the big screen. His first film was *No Way Out*. In it he played a doctor confronting racism. In *Blackboard Jungle* (1955), Poitier was a teacher at a tough inner-city school. Race was the central theme of 1958's *The Defiant Ones*. Poitier and white actor Tony Curtis starred as prisoners who escape from a work gang in the South—while chained together. Curtis's character is a raging racist, but he must work with Poitier's character to survive. The film earned Poitier a New York Film Critics' Best Actor award.

Poitier took a break from films to perform in the 1959 play *A Raisin in the Sun*.

Then, in 1961, he appeared in the film version of Lorraine Hansberry's acclaimed play.

ACADEMY AWARD WINNER

In 1963, Poitier played the lead role in *Lilies of the Field*. A small-budget movie, it was filmed in less than two weeks. The plot was simple. Yet Poitier brought a depth and complexity to his character, the traveling handyman Homer Smith. Poitier won Best Actor in a Leading Role honors at the 1964 Academy Awards. It was the first time an African American received a leading-actor Oscar.

Still, some African-American leaders were less than thrilled. They said the character of Homer bore too much of a resemblance to the "good slave" Uncle Tom. Homer's strong arms prove useful to a group of white people. And at the end of the movie, he learns from the whites he has helped.

The Plot of Lilies of the Field

A traveling handyman named Homer Smith is driving through the desert in the Southwest. He notices some nuns trying to fix a fence. He offers to do some work for them. He thinks they will pay him. But they don't have any money.

Mother Maria, the leader of the sisters, is tough. She helped the nuns escape from East Germany, where they climbed over the Berlin Wall. She thinks God has sent Homer to her.

The nuns want a chapel. Little by little, they convince the ex-soldier to build it for them. At first, people from the nearby town watch him. Then they start to help. Soon, Homer finishes the chapel. At the end of the film, he leaves, proud of the work he has done.

Actor Sidney Poitier shows off the special Oscar he received at the 2002 Academy Awards ceremony. The first African-American man to win an Oscar for Best Actor, Poitier's skill and charisma opened the way for many other black actors from the 1960s to the present day.

Other films in which Poitier starred would have more of an edge. In 1967's *Guess Who's Coming to Dinner*, he played the fiancé of a young white woman whose parents aren't happy about the interracial relationship. *In the Heat of the Night*, also released in 1967, had him portraying a homicide detective from Philadelphia, Pennsylvania, who is swept up in a murder investigation in a racist town in the South. These and other films caused moviegoers—white as well as black—to think about their own prejudices at a time when racial tensions were roiling American society.

At the 2002 Academy Awards ceremony, Sidney Poitier received a special Oscar for lifetime achievement. Poitier's long and distinguished career helped pave the way for other African-American actors. Fittingly, on the same night Poitier received his lifetime achievement award, the leading-role Oscars went to two black stars, Denzel Washington and Halle Berry.

DOING THE RIGHT THING: SPIKE LEE

One hundred years ago, the American movie industry was largely closed to blacks. Today, Hollywood's ranks are filled with talented African-American artists. Director Spike Lee is among the most influential. In a career spanning three decades and counting, Lee has released numerous noteworthy movies. These films can be challenging. Often, they are controversial. Lee takes an unblinking look at subjects many people would rather not think about. Some of his work has infuriated critics. But Lee cannot be ignored.

Shelton Jackson Lee was born in Atlanta, Georgia, on March 20, 1957. As a toddler, he was given the nickname Spike because he seemed tough and not afraid of anything. When he was young, his parents moved to New York City. His mother, Jacquelyn, was a teacher. His father, Bill, was a jazz musician. Both parents encouraged his interest in African-American art and culture.

Spike Lee attended a public high school in Brooklyn. After graduating, he went to Morehouse College as a mass communication major. Located in Atlanta, Morehouse is an all-male and historically black institution.

In 1977, Jacquelyn Lee died from cancer. Spike's friends, wanting to take his mind off his grief, frequently took him to movies. During this time,

Filmmaker Spike Lee has won many awards for his movies, which often deal with racial tensions and urban life.

Spike Lee concluded that Hollywood didn't understand African Americans. He decided to make more realistic films about black culture and communities.

After getting his undergraduate degree from Morehouse, Lee signed up for the graduate film program at New York University. He made a short film titled *Joe's Bed-Stuy Barbershop: We Cut Heads*. It won the 1983 Motion Picture Arts and Sciences' Student Academy Award.

In 1986, Lee released his first feature film, *She's Gotta Have It*. It was a comedy about men and women. In addition to directing the picture, Lee played a small role. African-American audiences loved it.

His next film, *School Daze*, was released in 1988. It was a musical comedy. Still, the movie included a very controversial theme: "colorism." Colorism involves African Americans treating one another differently based on how light or dark their skin is. Lee knew that many people in the African-American community would be angered that *School Daze* dealt with this issue. But he has never been one to shy away from an uncomfortable subject.

In *Do the Right Thing* (1989), Lee examined hatred and bigotry in a Brooklyn neighborhood. The film was nominated for an Academy Award for Best Original Screenplay.

Since then, Lee has made more than 200 films, television episodes, music videos, commercials, and documentaries. Originality, passion, and honesty continue to be hallmarks of his work.

In 2005, 67-year-old Morgan Freeman (left) became the oldest black actor to win an Academy Award (Best Supporting Actor, for *Million Dollar Baby*). That same year, Jamie Foxx became the first African-American actor—and only the second actor in history—to receive Oscar nominations for two different films (*Collateral* and *Ray*) in the same year. That year Foxx won the Academy Award for Best Actor for his portrayal of Ray Charles in *Ray*.

Oprah Winfrey is one of the most powerful people in the history of television entertainment. In 2011 she started her own television channel, the Oprah Winfrey Network.

5

ON THE SMALL SCREEN

L ike radio in its golden years, today's television broadcasts reach huge audiences. Although television broadcasts began in the late 1930s, TV sets were costly then. Most American families didn't get a television until the 1950s.

Black singers, dancers, and comics quickly found recognition on television. The first variety program on TV was *The Ed Sullivan Show*. It debuted in 1948. Among his guests, Sullivan showcased the talents of African-American entertainers. Steve Allen also hosted African-American stars on his *Tonight Show*.

It took longer for African-American actors to land dramatic roles on TV. In the late 1950s, things started to change. Several black performers, including Eartha Kitt, appeared on television dramas. In 1957, a Broadway play called *The Green Pastures* aired on TV. It had an all-black cast.

Many African-American comedians turned their painful personal experiences with racism into laughter. And television gave them the opportunity to reach a large audience.

NIPSEY RUSSELL: POET LAUREATE OF TV

One of the best-known African-American comedians on television was Nipsey Russell. He was born in Atlanta in 1918. When he was three years old, he tap-danced with a group. When he was 10, he saw the dancer and comedian Jack Wiggins. Wiggins wasn't a minstrel in blackface and ragged clothes. He was a dignified professional. Russell wanted to be like him.

Russell developed his skills as a teenager. He worked as a carhop at a drive-in. When he took people their food, he told jokes. They loved it and gave him big tips.

While in college, Russell studied classic literature and Old English. After college, he served as an army medic during World War II. When the war was over, he developed a nightclub act. He performed onstage in New York. He also made "party" record albums based on his routines.

Russell broke into TV with a 1957 appearance on *The Ed Sullivan Show*. A few years later, he landed a steady role as Officer Anderson on the popular situation comedy *Car 54: Where Are You?* From the 1960s through the 1990s, he appeared on a multitude of TV programs of all kinds—sitcoms, dramas, variety shows, talk shows, game shows. Over the years, his quick wit delighted countless viewers.

Comedians often have a specialty. Russell was known as "television's poet laureate." He used short verses and rhymes in his act. He knew hundreds of them by heart.

Nipsey Russell died on October 2, 2005. For almost 40 years, he had made people smile.

RICHARD PRYOR: "THE ROSA PARKS OF COMEDY"

Richard Pryor turned the pain of his life into stories. He made millions of people laugh. He also made them think.

Richard Pryor was born in Peoria, Illinois, on December 1, 1940. His family life was extremely troubled, and he had a difficult childhood. But as a young adolescent, he showed a rare gift for comedy. He performed in shows at a local recreation center.

At age 14, Pryor was expelled from school. He spent the next six years taking any job he could find. He worked as a shoe-shiner, a janitor, a drummer, a meat-packer, and a truck driver. Later, after serving in the army, he

decided to turn his comedic gifts into a career.

In 1963, Pryor went to New York. There, he started building a name for himself in comedy. Television discovered him in 1966. He appeared on *The Tonight Show*, *The Ed Sullivan Show*, and *The Merv Griffin Show*. He also did stand-up comedy onstage.

In his comedy, Pryor dealt with serious subjects such as racism and politics. He also drew on his troubled personal life, including his drug abuse, for material. His language was often coarse. But Pryor's comedy wasn't tinged with bitterness. It wasn't mean-spirited. Pryor found humanity even in terrible situations.

Many people consider Richard Pryor (1940–2005) to be the greatest comedian of all time. He had a successful TV career as both a writer and a performer, and also starred in many hit movies during the 1970s and 1980s.

In the early 1970s, Pryor wrote scripts for the TV sitcom *Sanford and Son* and *The Flip Wilson Show*, a half-hour variety series. He cowrote the screenplay for the film *Blazing Saddles* (1974), a madcap comedy from director Mel Brooks. Pryor would win an Emmy and a Writers Guild Award for his writing.

Pryor also had a successful acting career. He appeared in dozens of films and TV episodes. He hosted several television shows, including *Saturday Night Live*. Pryor won the NAACP Hall of Fame Award in 1996 for his performances. In 1998, he won the first Mark Twain Prize for American Humor.

Pryor had many health problems, some related to his heavy use of drugs and alcohol. For the last two decades of his life, he suffered from multiple sclerosis. He died on December 10, 2005.

Richard Pryor influenced many other African-American comedians,

including Eddie Murphy, Chris Rock, Steve Harvey, and Bernie Mac. Many white comedians have also acknowledged their debt to Pryor. These comics include Denis Leary and Jerry Seinfeld.

But Pryor's most significant legacy may be as a trailblazer for African Americans in the comedy genre. Chris Rock compared him with a pioneer of the civil rights movement. "Richard Pryor," Rock said, "was the Rosa Parks of comedy."

BILL COSBY: TV TRAILBLAZER

Another major African-American comedic star was Bill Cosby. He was born in Philadelphia on July 12, 1937. In elementary school, he learned to love sports. In high school, he spent too much time on athletics. He dropped out of school after repeating the 10th grade.

Cosby joined the U.S. Navy and got his high school diploma by mail.

Bill Cosby became known as a master at telling humorous stories as a stand-up comedian in the 1960s and 1970s. He had many successes as a television writer, producer, and actor, but probably his greatest accomplishment was the hit sitcom *The Cosby Show*. It was the top-rated show of the 1980s, and its success opened the way for other programs on mainstream television about African Americans.

When his tour of duty ended, he enrolled at Temple University. To earn money, he worked in a bar at night. He made customers laugh.

In the early 1960s, Cosby started doing stand-up comedy in clubs. Audiences all over the country loved the stories he told about his days growing up in Philadelphia. Cosby had a special way of telling stories. He said he learned it from jazz greats like Miles Davis. He took an idea, and then found different ways to express it.

Cosby made a major breakthrough in 1965. He became the first African American to play a lead role in a dramatic television series. The name of the show was *I Spy*. Cosby won three Emmy Awards for his work on the show. *I Spy* was cancelled after the 1968 season, but for Cosby other TV series would follow.

One was the Saturday morning children's show *Fat Albert and the Cosby Kids*. Cosby hosted the program, which included animated and live-action segments. He also voiced many of the cartoon characters. *Fat Albert and the Cosby Kids*, which debuted in 1972, was groundbreaking. Never before had a cartoon show focused on African-American characters. But *Fat Albert* appealed to children of all backgrounds. It ran until 1985.

The previous year, Cosby had launched another landmark series. This one, a sitcom called *The Cosby Show*, aired in prime time. The series centered on the Huxtables, an African-American family living in New York City. But unlike any previous African-American family depicted on TV, the Huxtables were well-to-do professionals. The father, Cliff (played by Cosby), was a doctor. The mother, Clair, was a lawyer. Their children were smart and well adjusted. Civil rights leader Coretta Scott King hailed *The Cosby Show* as "the most positive portrayal of black family life that has ever been broadcast."

The Cosby Show was the most popular sitcom of the 1980s. It won six Emmys and more than 40 other awards during its eight-year run.

NICHELLE NICHOLS: INSPIRATION FROM THE 23RD CENTURY

In 1966, Nichelle Nichols took the role of Lieutenant Uhura on *Star Trek*. This was a first. Never before had a black actress played a character other than a servant on a major TV series.

In a *Star Trek* episode that originally aired in November 1968, Nichols was involved in another first. She kissed co-star William Shatner. Never before had a black person shared a kiss with a white person on American TV. For some people, the kiss seemed to offer hope that race relations in American society might improve.

After the original *Star Trek* television series was cancelled, Nichelle Nichols played the part of Lieutenant Uhura in seven films.

Nichols had wanted to leave *Star Trek* after the show's first season. The Chicago native wanted to go back to musical theater, where she'd gotten her start in show business. But Nichols met the great civil rights leader Martin Luther King Jr. at an NAACP dinner. King confessed that he was a big fan of hers. When Nichols mentioned her plans to leave *Star Trek*, King urged her to reconsider. Her work, he said, was important for African Americans. She portrayed a strong black character—and in a fictional universe where race didn't define a person's identity. She was, in short, a role model.

King, it seems, was right about Nichols being a role model. Many people would later say that the actress and her character Lt. Uhura inspired them. Among these people was Dr. Mae C. Jemison. Jemison became America's first black female astronaut.

In the 1970s, after the original *Star Trek* series was cancelled, Nichelle Nichols moved to Houston to work for NASA, the U.S. space agency. She was in charge of finding women and minorities to be astronauts. She worked with many talented people, including Sally Ride (the first woman in space), Guion Bluford (the first African-American male astronaut), Judith Resnik, and Ronald McNair.

TALK SHOWS MAKE AN IMPACT

Some of the most influential African Americans on television have worked as talk show hosts. The most famous talk show host of all time is Oprah Winfrey. She was born January 29, 1954, in Kosciusko, Mississippi. As a teenager, she left her mother's home in a Mississippi farming town and joined her father in Nashville, Tennessee. The city offered many opportunities. She found a job at a local radio station.

In 1971, she enrolled in Tennessee State University. She majored in speech at the all-black college.

In 1976, Winfrey hosted her first television show, *People Are Talking*, in Baltimore. After eight years, she moved to Illinois to do *A.M. Chicago*. Within a few months, it rocketed to number one in its time slot. Winfrey gained national recognition.

Oprah Winfrey holds the People's Choice Award for Favorite Talk Show Host that she won in 2004. Oprah was the first African American to become a billionaire. Today *Forbes* magazine estimates her net worth at about $3 billion.

In 1985, Steven Spielberg cast her in *The Color Purple*, his film adaptation of the Alice Walker novel. Winfrey was nominated for an Academy Award and a Golden Globe for her work in the movie.

The next year, she launched *The Oprah Winfrey Show*. In its first year, the talk show had a nationwide audience of 10 million people. Winfrey had a simple secret: she acted like a best friend to her audience members. Her show's success was phenomenal. When Oprah featured books, her selections became instant bestsellers. Every diet she tried swept the country. Her Miracle Network raised more than $51 million for charity.

In 1999, Winfrey helped establish a cable and Internet company called Oxygen Media. It focused on programming for women. She started her own magazine for women, *O: The Oprah Magazine*, a year later. On January 1, 2011, she launched the Oprah Winfrey Network (OWN).

One of the richest and most influential people in the United States, Winfrey continues to touch the lives of millions every day. Her long-running talk show finally ended in 2011.

OTHER TALK SHOW HOSTS

Following in Oprah's famous footsteps, Tyra Banks, a supermodel, started a talk show in 2005. *The Tyra Banks Show* target-

Supermodel Tyra Banks has created several popular television shows, including the long-running program *America's Next Top Model* and her talk show *The Tyra Banks Show*, which aired from 2005 to 2010.

ed young women. It ran until 2010. Banks also created a popular reality show for aspiring models, called *America's Next Top Model*. It debuted in 2003 and was still on the air as of 2012.

Montel Williams, an inspirational speaker, started his own talk show in 1991. *The Montel Williams Show* ran for 17 years and covered many topics. Williams often stressed the importance of family and education in his shows. His favorite shows were about teens and relationships. In his book, *Mountain, Get Out of My Way*, Williams wrote, "I'm in it to make a difference, to change the world, one viewer at a time."

MINISERIES AND DOCUMENTARIES

Television has made African-American history come alive through specials, documentaries, and miniseries. One of the most famous of these aired in 1977. It was the miniseries *Roots*, based on a book by Alex Haley. The miniseries ran for eight nights. The story followed the life of a black man, Kunta Kinte, and his descendants. It began in 1750 with Kunta Kinte's birth in Africa. Viewers

— *Did You Know?* —

Roots was nominated for 36 Emmy Awards, winning 9.

watched as he was sold into slavery and brought to America. The brutal reality of slavery was made personal and real.

Since then, countless documentaries have explored topics related to the African-American experience. These include award-winning programs about jazz music, the civil rights movement, and the aftermath of Hurricane Katrina in New Orleans.

*   *   *   *   *

Over the past 150 years, African Americans have played an increasingly prominent role in the entertainment business. As producers, screenwriters, directors, playwrights, actors, and comedians, they have enriched American culture.

CHAPTER NOTES

p. 10: "Don't go to see this . . ." *New York Age*, quoted in Langston Hughes and Milton Meltzer, *Black Magic: A Pictorial History of the Negro in American Entertainment* (New Jersey: Prentice-Hall, Inc., 1967), p. 230.

p. 11: "I think it will help . . ." Lorraine Hansberry, *To Be Young, Gifted and Black: Lorraine Hansberry in Her Own Words* (New York: Signet Classics, 2011), p. 109.

p. 12: "I knew for certain . . ." Sidney Poitier, *The Measure of a Man: A Spiritual Autobiography* (New York: HarperCollins Publishers, 2000), p. 179.

p. 12: "One line in the play . . ." Louis Gossett Jr., *An Actor and a Gentleman* (Hoboken, NJ: John Wiley and Sons, 2010), p. 84.

p. 19: "the funniest man I ever. . ." W. C. Fields, quoted in Hughes and Meltzer, *Black Magic*, p. 54.

p. 21: "When we picture . . ." Bert Williams, quoted in Camille F. Forbes, *Introducing Bert Williams: Burnt Cork, Broadway, and the Story of America's First Black Star* (New York: Basic Civitas Books, 2008), p. 172.

p. 21: "Companies of purposeful players . . ." Ibid., p. 172.

p. 23: "Bert Williams has done more . . ." Booker T. Washington, quoted in *Harlem Renaissance Lives*, edited by Henry Louis Gates and Evelyn Brooks Higginbotham (New York: Oxford University Press, 2009), p. 534.

p. 24: "The extraordinary achievements . . ." Paul Robeson Jr., "Voice of a Century," *Black Collegian*, vol. 41, issue 1 (September 2010), p. 40.

p. 30: "I can be a maid . . ." Hattie McDaniel, quoted in Jill Watts, *Hattie McDaniel: Black Ambition, White Hollywood* (New York: Amistad, 2007), p. 139.

p. 32: "You're a comedian," quoted in "Duffy's Tavern," *Ebony* vol. 4, no. 5 (March 1949), p. 26.

p. 32: "We have to get in . . ." Eddie Green, quoted in "Duffy's Tavern," p. 26.

p. 32:   "At one time I wanted . . ." Richard Goldstein, "Art Rust Jr., Pioneer in Sports Talk Radio, Dies at 82," *New York Times* (January 13, 2010). http://www.nytimes.com/2010/01/14/sports/14rust.html

p. 37:   "black males in Hollywood . . ." Donald Bogle, *Toms, Coons, Mulattoes, Mammies, & Bucks: An Interpretive History of Blacks in American Films*, 4th edition (New York: The Continuum International Publishing Group, Inc., 2009), p.16.

p. 50:   "Richard Pryor was the Rosa . . ." Chris Rock, quoted in Jesse McKinley, "Admiration for a Comedian Who Knew No Limits," *New York Times*, December 13, 2005. http://www.nytimes.com/2005/12/13/arts/13pryo.html

p. 51:   "the most positive portrayal . . ." Coretta Scott King, quoted in "Bill Cosby" at Explore the Arts: The John F. Kennedy Center for the Performing Arts website. http://www.kennedy-center.org/explorer/artists/?entity_id=3713&source_type=A

p. 55:   "I'm in it to make . . ." Montel Williams, *Mountain, Get Out of My Way: Life Lessons and Learned Truths* (Thorndike, ME: Thorndike Press, 1996) p. 217.

CHRONOLOGY

1821	James Hewlett plays Othello at the African Grove Theater in New York City.
1851	Harriet Beecher Stowe's novel *Uncle Tom's Cabin* is published. It will become the basis for "Tom shows."
1910	Bert Williams becomes the first African-American entertainer in the Ziegfeld Follies.
1915	The NAACP protests the opening of *The Birth of a Nation*.
1919	Oscar Micheaux makes his first film, *The Homesteader*.
1924	Paul Robeson stars in Eugene O'Neill's play *All God's Chillun Got Wings*.
1939	Hattie McDaniel receives the Academy Award for Best Actress in a Supporting Role. She is the first African-American Oscar winner.
1959	*A Raisin in the Sun*, by Lorraine Hansberry, opens on Broadway.
1963	Sidney Poitier stars in *Lilies of the Field*, for which he wins the Academy Award for Best Actor in a Leading Role.
1965	Bill Cosby becomes the first African American to play a lead role in a dramatic series, *I Spy*.
1966	Nichelle Nichols becomes the first black actress in a major TV series to play a character who is not a servant. She portrays Lt. Uhura in *Star Trek*.
1986	Spike Lee's first feature film, *She's Gotta Have It*, opens.
1998	Richard Pryor receives the first Mark Twain Prize for American Humor.
2001	Denzel Washington becomes the second African-American actor to win the Oscar for Best Actor in a Leading Role. He is honored for his work in *Training Day*. Halle Berry becomes the first black actress to win the Academy Award for Best Actress in a Leading Role. She wins for *Monster's Ball*.
2004	Jamie Foxx wins the Best Actor Oscar for his portrayal of musician Ray Charles in the film *Ray*.
2006	Forest Whitaker wins the Academy Award for Best Actor. He played an African dictator in *The Last King of Scotland*.
2011	The last episode of *The Oprah Winfrey Show* airs.

GLOSSARY

abolitionist—a person who favored the ending of slavery.

blackface—dark makeup worn by an entertainer (often a white performer) portraying a black person.

discrimination—unfair treatment of people on the basis of their race, ethnicity, religion, or some other group characteristic.

distributor—a company or person who takes a product from its creator to the point of sale. A film distributor helps studios place their pictures in theaters.

minstrel—a member of a troupe of entertainers that performed comic skits, songs, and dances, in an exaggerated African-American style and often while wearing blackface, during the 19th and early 20th centuries.

pantomime—a kind of entertainment in which the performer tells a story (often a comic one) without using words.

producer—a person whose main job is to arrange financing for a play, film, or television show.

restrictive covenant—a legal agreement or promise written into deeds for houses or other property limiting their use or sale.

segregation—the practice of keeping people of different races separated.

stereotype—a commonly held belief that members of a large group of people (for example, African Americans) will tend to have the same abilities or behave in the same way.

troupe—a group of performers.

understudy—an actor who is not a regular cast member in a play but who studies a role so that he or she can fill in if the regular actor is unable to perform.

valet—a male servant who performs personal services (such as taking care of clothing) for a man.

vaudeville—a kind of variety show that flourished in the first decades of the 20th century.

FURTHER READING

Cooper, Ilene. *Up Close: Oprah Winfrey*. London: Puffin, 2008.

Hansberry, Lorraine. *To Be Young, Gifted and Black: Lorraine Hansberry in her Own Words*. Adapted by Robert Nemiroff. New York: Signet Classics, 2011.

Hughes, Langston, and Milton Meltzer. *Black Magic: A Pictorial History of the Negro in American Entertainment*. Upper Saddle River, NJ: Prentice-Hall, Inc., 1967.

Poitier, Sidney. *The Measure of a Man: A Spiritual Autobiography*. New York: HarperCollins Publishers, 2000.

Smith, Ronald L. *Cosby: The Life of a Comedy Legend*. Amherst, NY: Prometheus Books, 1997.

Watts, Jill. *Hattie McDaniel: Black Ambition, White Hollywood*. New York: Amistad, 2005.

INTERNET RESOURCES

http://www.biography.com/people/groups/famous-black-entertainers/

This site offers biographies of notable African-American entertainers.

http://www.pbs.org/wnet/americanmasters/episodes/paul-robeson/about-the-actor/66/

Companion website for the PBS *American Masters* profile of Paul Robeson.

http://www.imdb.com/name/nm0000490/

The Internet Movie Database is a great resource for those who want to find out about the work of a particular actor or director. The link above is for the IMDb's Spike Lee page.

http://www.talkinbroadway.com/world/RaisinSun.html

This site provides excellent reviews of Broadway plays. The link leads to a review of the 2004 production of *A Raisin in the Sun*.

http://shorock.com/arts/micheaux/

This outstanding site provides a wealth of information about the pioneering African-American filmmaker Oscar Micheaux.

http://www.museum.tv/eotvsection.php?entrycode=roots

Find out more about the groundbreaking miniseries *Roots* at the Museum of Broadcast Communications. Other important shows are also profiled on the site.

INDEX

Numbers in **bold italics** refer to captions.

CONTRIBUTORS

LINDA ARMSTRONG has a Bachelor of Arts degree in English and holds a lifetime California State Standard Teaching Credential. She taught third, fifth, and sixth grades before taking a position as Language Development Resource Teacher in the school library. She now writes educational materials and children's books.

Senior Consulting Editor **DR. MARC LAMONT HILL** is one of the leading hip-hop generation intellectuals in the country. Dr. Hill has lectured widely and provides regular commentary for media outlets like NPR, the *Washington Post, Essence Magazine*, the *New York Times*, CNN, MSNBC, and *The O'Reilly Factor*. He is the host of the nationally syndicated television show *Our World With Black Enterprise*. Dr. Hill is a columnist and editor-at-large for the *Philadelphia Daily News*. His books include the award-winning *Beats, Rhymes, and Classroom Life: Hip-Hop Pedagogy and the Politics of Identity* (2009).

Since 2009 Dr. Hill has been on the faculty of Columbia University as Associate Professor of Education at Teachers College. He holds an affiliated faculty appointment in African American Studies at the Institute for Research in African American Studies at Columbia University.

Since his days as a youth in Philadelphia, Dr. Hill has been a social justice activist and organizer. He is a founding board member of My5th, a non-profit organization devoted to educating youth about their legal rights and responsibilities. He is also a board member and organizer of the Philadelphia Student Union. Dr. Hill also works closely with the ACLU Drug Reform Project, focusing on drug informant policy. In addition to his political work, Dr. Hill continues to work directly with African American and Latino youth.

In 2005, *Ebony* named Dr. Hill one of America's 100 most influential Black leaders. The magazine had previously named him one of America's top 30 Black leaders under 30 years old.